How Do Planes Fly?
How Airplanes Work
Children's Aviation Books

PROFESSOR GUSTO
EDUCATIONAL & INFORMATIVE BOOKS FOR CHILDREN
(PRE-K / K-12)

Do you ever wonder how airplanes fly? Read on and discover!

The secrets
to flight are
in the wings.

As an airplane's engines start, the wings split the air flow. Some air flows above the wings while some air flows under the wings.

The air above the wings flows fast while the air under the wings flows slowly.

Plane wings have to be curved on top but flat on the bottom.

With the plane wings' structure, the wind above and below travel in different paths.

The difference in path creates lower air pressure above the wings as compared to the wind below them.

The high air pressure below the wings lifts the plane from above the ground. This force is called Lift.

The Weight is the force created by gravity to pull the plane toward the center of the Earth.

If the force of Lift is greater than Weight, the airplane moves upward.

Once there is enough lift to defy gravity, the airplane takes off.

Every time the airplane is in flight, the plane is slowed down by the air as it pushes on the plane. This is called Drag.

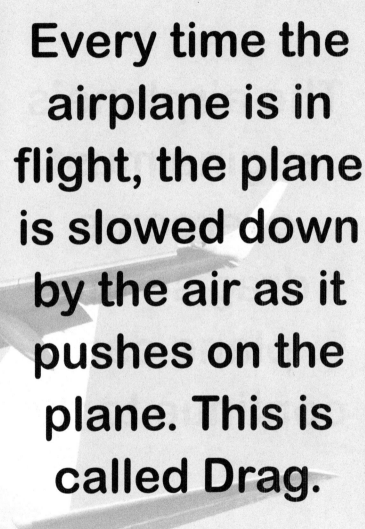

The airplane's engine must overcome drag so the plane can continue to fly.

The airplane's main weapon against drag is called thrust.

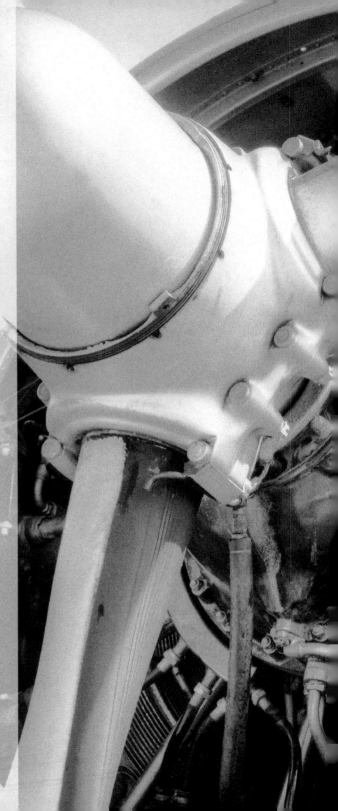

Thrust is the force produced by the engine usually found in front or in the wings of the airplane.

When the Thrust is greater than the force of Drag, the airplane moves forward.

Quick note: the airplane must move forward before it moves upward.

To sum up: the four forces to make airplanes fly are Weight, Lift, Thrust and Drag.

Did you enjoy learning how airplanes fly? Share this book with your friends!

CPSIA information can be obtained
at www.ICGtesting.com
Printed in the USA
LVOW05s1540030118
561661LV00005B/33/P